In Loving Memory of my father,

Jesse Lowery

CHEERS TO ALL
THE BOURBONITES!

Copyright © 2023
Bird House Publishing
8325 Broadway Street, Pearland, TX 77581

All rights reserved. No part of this book may be reproduced, stored, or transmitted by any means – whether auditory, graphic, mechanical, or electronic – without written permission of the author, except in the case of brief excerpts used in critical articles and reviews. Unauthorized reproduction of any part of this work is illegal and punishable by law.

ISBN: 979-8-9855113-6-9

Because of the dynamic nature of the internet, any web addresses or links contained in this book may have changed since publication and may no longer be valid. The views expressed in this work are solely those of the author and do not necessarily reflect the views of the publisher, and the publisher hereby disclaims any responsibility for them.

The publisher is not responsible for any health or allergy needs that may require medical supervision. The publisher is not responsible for any adverse reactions to recipes or ingredients contained in this book. Please enjoy any alcoholic beverages safely and do not operate vehicles or heavy machinery while under the influence.

Bird House Publishing rev date 01/07/23

THE
CLASSIC

INTRODUCTION

Hey Bourbonites, it's the Old Fashioned Barrister, and I wrote a cocktail book! For those who do not know me, let me introduce myself. I am the Old Fashioned Barrister. I am a Texas lawyer (barrister) who loves old-fashioned cocktails, whiskey, and bourbon. You may be asking yourself, *why is a lawyer writing a cocktail book? Does this lawyer have experience mixing cocktails?* The answer to the second question is no. As for the first question, I decided to write this book to share my favorite cocktail and its variations with you.

I also wrote this book because I want to inspire people who are sitting on their passions and gifts, feel stuck in their careers, and have told themselves that there is no way out.

I am you! I am a burnt-out family law attorney who woke up one day and decided to take control of my life. I am a fed-up licensed practicing attorney of ten years who decided to step out on faith and do something entirely out of the norm. I am an unappreciated employee who decided to take my passion and spread it with others.

This cocktail book is for those who are dreamers but feel they do not know where to start. This cocktail book is for novices and enthusiasts of the whiskey community. It is meant to introduce various spins on the classic old-fashioned and for those who like to entertain and show off for friends and family. This book is for those who are tired of spending money at establishments that make subpar old-fashioneds.

This book is for those who like to experiment and have fun mixing cocktails. You don't have to be a mixologist or a bartender. This book aims to bring you into my world, which is outside of the practice of law and show my love for old-fashioned bourbon and whiskey.

Throughout this book, I provide my Bourbon & Bits, interesting information about the world of bourbon. I hope you enjoy this book as much as I enjoyed writing it. This book is made with love and fun! Cheers!

*"TOO MUCH OF ANYTHING IS BAD,
BUT TOO MUCH GOOD WHISKEY IS BARELY ENOUGH."*

– MARK TWAIN

COCKTAIL | CONTENTS

5	Introduction
7	The Classic
15	Smoke This B*tch
23	Just Call Me Old Fashioned
57	Let's Get Festive
73	Old Fashioned With a Twist
95	I'm Just Here for the Drinks
130	References

When writing a cocktail book about old-fashioneds, you must start with *"The Classic Old Fashioned."* I was introduced to this cocktail while on a trip to New Orleans. At a bar with some friends, one suggested I needed to try this drink. During this time in my life, I was still trying to figure out what I wanted my go-to signature drink to be. As a lawyer, I needed a classic, sophisticated, and sexy drink that would be a conversation piece.

My friend ordered the drink, and I was impressed with how the bartender made it. He put all ingredients in a mixing glass. After stirring, he poured my drink into a rock glass, lit the orange peel with a lighter, lined the rim, and then dropped it in my glass. After witnessing that, this has become my go-to cocktail and favorite.

I can say that since I have been drinking *"The Classic Old Fashioned,"* I have seen and tasted it in different ways. I've tried it with club soda or water called a *Wisconsin Old Fashioned*. I have tried it with muddled cherries and oranges. I have tried it with a red cherry instead of a Luxardo cherry, and I have also tried it with simple syrup, granulated sugar, or sugar cubes. After trying these different variations, my favorite way of drinking an old-fashioned is with simple syrup without the water or club soda, no muddling of the cherries and oranges, and a Luxardo cherry with an added orange peel.

BOURBON & BITS

The old-fashioned cocktail was first created in Louisville, KY, at the Pendennis Club, a gentleman's club founded in 1881. A bartender at the club made it in honor of Col. James E Pepper, a prominent bourbon distiller. Col. Pepper took the recipe to the Waldorf Astoria Hotel in New York. The recipe was first published in 1895 in a book called Modern American Drinks by George Kappeler. Now, June 14 is observed as National Old Fashioned Day.

THE CLASSIC OLD FASHIONED

Ingredients

2 oz Maker's Mark Kentucky Straight Bourbon Whisky or your favorite whiskey

2 dashes of Angostura Bitters

½ oz of simple syrup

Orange peel

1 Luxardo cherry

Mixing Method

1. Mix the Maker's Mark Kentucky Straight Bourbon Whisky, bitters, and simple syrup in a mixing glass.
2. Stir well for 5 to 15 seconds.
3. Pour into a rock glass over a round or square ice cube.
4. Rub the orange peel around the rim of the glass and then place the orange peel in the glass.
5. Garnish with a Luxardo cherry.

Tips

You can create your simple syrup if you feel creative and adventurous. Add 3–4 sugar cubes or 3–4 teaspoons of sugar into boiling water. Stir until it thickens.

SMOKE THIS B*TCH

You may wonder why I titled this section of the book *"Smoke This B*TCH."* Well, as you probably have seen recently, smoked cocktails are making their rounds in the spirit community, especially with old-fashioneds. I love a good, smoked old-fashioned, so I enjoy adding a flavor of wood chips to my smoker and smoking them with my torch. I enjoy seeing the smoke coming out of my glass and the smoked aroma that it brings to my drink.

However, you will have friends and family who are not fans of this concept, which is okay. As you prepare to light that b*tch up and smoke your old-fashioned, show them another section of this book. I promise you there is something for everyone in this book. Have fun and get smokey!

BOURBON & BITS

Eben Freeman, a native New Yorker and cocktails consultant, created the first smoked cocktail in 2007. He made "Waylon." He states, "it tastes like a bourbon and Coke when consumed beside a smoker full of ribs."

SMOKED OLD FASHIONED

Ingredients

2 oz whiskey

2 dashes of Angostura Bitters

½ oz of simple syrup

1 orange peel

1 Luxardo cherry

Mixing Method

1. Mix the whiskey, bitters, and simple syrup in a mixing glass.
2. Stir well for 5 to 15 seconds.
3. Pour into a rock glass over a round or square ice cube.
4. Rub the orange peel around the rim of the glass and then place the orange peel in the glass.
5. Garnish with Luxardo cherry.
6. Place your smoker on top of the rock glass. Add flavored wood chips to your smoker. Light your wood chips for 30 to 45 seconds. Stand back and let it smoke.

Tips

If you have a smoke box, you do not need to use flavored wood chips.

JUST CALL ME OLD FASHIONED

While drinking old-fashioneds, I noticed that the classic has changed. You can turn your classic old-fashioned into whatever flavor that you like it to be by adding flavored bitters and syrups or adding extra ounces of whiskey.

This section will provide you with different ways to experiment with the flavors, sweetnesses, or spices to add to your old-fashioned. Your cocktail can still be classic and sophisticated, but it doesn't hurt to stir things up a bit.

BUTTERSCOTCH OLD FASHIONED

CHOCOLATE OLD FASHIONED

CHOCOLATE PECAN OLD FASHIONED

CRANBERRY ORANGE OLD FASHIONED

DAN'S APPLEJACK OLD FASHIONED

FRENCH HIBISCUS OLD FASHIONED

JALAPENO OLD FASHIONED

MAPLE OLD FASHIONED

ORANGE OLD FASHIONED

PEACH OLD FASHIONED

PEANUT BUTTER OLD FASHIONED

PLUM OLD FASHIONED

VANILLA OLD FASHIONED

BOURBON & BITS

Tom Bullock was the first African American bartender to author and publish a cocktail book called *"The Ideal Bartender."* The book was published during the pre-Prohibition era. He also contributed to the creation of the old-fashioned while working at the Pendennis Club.

BUTTERSCOTCH OLD FASHIONED

Ingredients

2 oz whiskey

2 dashes of Angostura Orange Bitters

½ oz butterscotch schnapps

½ oz vanilla extract

Mixing Method

1. Mix the whiskey, bitters, and butterscotch schnapps in a mixing glass.
2. Stir well for 5 to 15 seconds.
3. Pour into a rock glass over a round or square ice cube.

Tips

Use any brand of butterscotch schnapps of your choice.

CHOCOLATE OLD FASHIONED

Ingredients

2 oz G-Man Bourbon Whiskey

2 dashes of Fee Brothers Chocolate Bitters

½ oz of simple syrup

1 Luxardo cherry

Mixing Method

1. Mix the whiskey, chocolate bitters, and simple syrup in a mixing glass.
2. Stir well for 5 to 15 seconds.
3. Pour into a rock glass over a round or square ice cube.
4. Garnish with a Luxardo cherry and a small chocolate chunk bar of your choice.

BOURBON & BITS

G-Man Bourbon Whiskey is distilled in Lawrenceburg, Indiana. The bourbon is aged in Lawrenceburg for up to four years. Then the barrels are transported to a distillery in Jacksonville, Florida, where the bourbon continues to age until it meets their high standards for bottling. To purchase a bottle, visit their website at https://gmanbourbon.com/.

CHOCOLATE PECAN OLD FASHIONED

Ingredients

2½ oz Standard Proof Pecan Rye Whiskey

4 dashes of Fee Brothers Aztec Chocolate Bitters

½ oz of simple syrup

Mixing Method

1. Mix the whiskey, bitters, and simple syrup in a mixing glass.
2. Stir well for 5 to 10 seconds.
3. Pour into a rock glass over a round or square ice cube.

Tips

Standard Proof Pecan Rye Whiskey is a flavored Tennessee made in Nashville, Tennessee. To purchase a bottle, please go to their website https://www.standardproofwhiskey.com/.

This cocktail was created by Houston attorney Dan Scarbrough

CRANBERRY ORANGE OLD FASHIONED

Ingredients

2 oz whiskey

3 dashes Angostura Orange Bitters

3 dashes Fee Brothers Cranberry Bitters

½ oz simple syrup

1 orange peel

1 cranberry

Mixing Method

1. Mix the whiskey, bitters, and simple syrup in a mixing glass.
2. Stir well for 5 to 15 seconds.
3. Pour into a rock glass over a round or square ice cube.
4. Rub the orange peel around the rim of the glass, then place the orange peel in the glass.
5. Garnish with the orange peel and cranberry.

Image by KamranAydinov on Freepik

DAN'S APPLEJACK OLD FASHIONED

Ingredients

2 oz Laird's Applejack Whiskey

3 dashes of Peychaud's Aromatic Bitters

½ oz of simple syrup

Mixing Method

1. Mix the whiskey, bitters, and simple syrup in a mixing glass.
2. Stir well for 5 to 15 seconds.
3. Pour into a rock glass over a round or square ice cube.

This cocktail was created by Houston attorney Dan Scarbrough

FRENCH HIBISCUS OLD FASHIONED

Ingredients

2 oz Maker's Mark French Oaked 46

2 dashes of cardamom bitters

2 Wild Hibiscus Rose Syrup Flowers

¼ oz of simple syrup

¼ oz hibiscus syrup

Mixing Method

1. Mix the Maker's Mark French Oaked 46, bitters, simple syrup, and hibiscus syrup in a mixing glass.
2. Stir well for 5 to 10 seconds.
3. Pour into a rock glass over a round or square ice cube.
4. Garnish with the Wild Hibiscus Rose Syrup Flowers

This cocktail was created by Houston attorney Dan Scarbrough

Image by stockking on Freepik

JALAPENO OLD FASHIONED

Ingredients

2 ½ oz G-Man Bourbon Whiskey

2 dashes of Angostura Bitters

½ oz of simple syrup

1 small jalapeno pepper, seeded

Mixing Method

1. Cut ½ of the jalapeno pepper into 2 or 3 slices (depending on your level of spice).
2. Muddle the sliced jalapeno peppers into the glass.
3. Mix the whiskey, bitters, muddled jalapeno peppers, and simple syrup in a mixing glass.
4. Stir well for 5 to 15 seconds.
5. Pour into a rock glass over a round or square ice cube.
6. Garnish with jalapeno and an orange peel.

MAPLE OLD FASHIONED

Ingredients

2 oz Knob Creek Smoked Maple Kentucky Straight Bourbon Whiskey

4 dashes of Fee Brothers Black Walnut Bitters

2 tablespoons of simple syrup

Mixing Method

1. Mix the whiskey, bitters, and simple syrup in a mixing glass.
2. Stir well for 5 to 15 seconds.
3. Pour into a rock glass over a round or square ice cube.

ORANGE OLD FASHIONED

Ingredients

2 oz G-Man Bourbon Whiskey

2 dashes of Angostura Orange Bitters

½ oz of simple syrup

1 orange peel

1 Luxardo cherry

Mixing Method

1. Mix the whiskey, bitters, and simple syrup in a mixing glass.
2. Stir well for 5 to 15 seconds.
3. Pour into a rock glass over a round or square ice cube.
4. Rub the orange peel around the rim of the glass, then place the orange peel in the glass.
5. Garnish with a Luxardo cherry and orange peel.

PEACH OLD FASHIONED

Ingredients

2 oz G-Man Bourbon Whiskey

3–4 dashes of peach bitters

¾ oz of simple syrup

1 peach slice

Mixing Method

1. Mix the whiskey, bitters, and simple syrup in a mixing glass.
2. Stir well for 5 to 15 seconds.
3. Pour into a rock glass over a round or square ice cube.
4. Rub the peach peel around the rim of the glass, then place the peach peel in the glass.
5. Garnish with a peach slice.

Tips

If you like a smokey flavor, this cocktail can be smoked. Add the oak flavor wood chips to enhance the flavor.

PEANUT BUTTER OLD FASHIONED

Ingredients

2 oz Screwball Whiskey

2 dashes Fee Brothers Aztec Chocolate Bitters

2 tablespoons simple syrup

1 orange peel

Mixing Method

1. Mix the whiskey, bitters, and simple syrup in a mixing glass.
2. Stir well for 5 to 15 seconds.
3. Pour into a rock glass over a round or square of ice.
4. Rub the orange peel around the rim of the glass, then place the orange peel in the glass.
5. Garnish with an orange peel.

PLUM OLD FASHIONED

Ingredients

2 oz whiskey

2–3 dashes of Fee Brothers Plum Bitters

½ oz of simple syrup

1 orange peel

1 Luxardo cherry

Mixing Method

1. Mix the whiskey, bitters, and simple syrup in a mixing glass.
2. Stir well for 5 to 15 seconds.
3. Pour into a rock glass over a round or square ice cube.
4. Rub the orange peel around the rim of the glass, then place the orange peel in the glass.
5. Garnish with a Luxardo cherry and orange peel.

VANILLA OLD FASHIONED

Ingredients

2 oz Maker's Mark Kentucky Straight Bourbon Whisky

2 dashes of Fee Brothers Chocolate Bitters

½ oz of vanilla extract

Mixing Method

1. Mix the whiskey, bitters, and simple syrup in a mixing glass.
2. Stir well for 5 to 10 seconds.
3. Pour into a rock glass over a round or square ice cube.

This cocktail was created by Houston attorney Dan Scarbrough

LET'S GET FESTIVE

My favorite seasons are fall and winter, and I love celebrating the holidays! For me, holidays mean fall festivals, holiday warmth, and football season! I am a huge Dallas Cowboys fan, and, being a Dallas native, I was raised as one. What's football without a good cocktail?

During these times of the year, I enjoy drinking anything made with warm flavors. Also, it's fun to get creative by mixing up festive cocktails during the holiday seasons. In this section, I have provided various holiday fun and festive old-fashioneds.

You can fall in love with pumpkin or cinnamon spice and everything nice. Have a winter wonderland with peppermint and cranberry, or sip with your Galentines or the person who chose you during the "cuffing" season. However you prefer to spruce up your festive old-fashioned, make sure you make it lively!

CINNAMON SPICED CRANBERRY OLD FASHIONED

CUPID'S WHISKEY EGGNOG OLD FASHIONED

PEPPERMINT OLD FASHIONED

PUMPKIN SPICE OLD FASHIONED

BOURBON & BITS

All bourbon is whiskey, but not all whiskey is bourbon. Bourbon has specific requirements that make it a bourbon. The criteria for bourbon are (1) it is aged in a new, charred, white oak barrel, (2) it is made in America, (3) it has at least 51% corn, (4) it is distilled at less than 160 proof (5) it is at 80 proof or higher at final proof going into the bottle, and (6) it has no artificial flavors or colors.

CINNAMON SPICED CRANBERRY OLD FASHIONED

Ingredients

2 oz King's Creek Black Label Cider Whiskey

3 dashes of cranberry bitters

½ oz of simple syrup

1 cinnamon stick

Mixing Method

1. Mix the infused King's Creek Black Label Cider Whiskey, bitters, and simple syrup in a mixing glass.
2. Stir well for 5 to 15 seconds.
3. Pour into a rock glass over a round or square ice cube.
4. Garnish with a cinnamon stick. Adding a cranberry is optional.

Tips

To infuse King's Creek Black Labe Cider Whiskey, insert two to three cinnamon sticks in the whiskey bottle. Allow the cinnamon sticks to soak in the bottle for about two to three days. Taste the whiskey and if it is to your liking, begin using it. If you like, you can allow it to sit for a few more days for your taste.

CUPID'S WHISKEY VALENTINE'S & GALENTINE'S COCKTAIL

Ingredients

2 oz Skrewball Whiskey

1 oz cranberry juice of your choice

½ oz Grand Marnier

Mixing Method

1. Add whiskey, cranberry juice, and Grand Marnier in a cocktail shaker filled with ice.
2. Shake the well for 10 to 20 seconds.
3. Strain over ice in any glass you prefer.

EGGNOG OLD FASHIONED

Ingredients

2 oz eggnog

1 oz of whiskey

½ vanilla extract

1–2 dashes of Angostura bitters

1 cinnamon stick

Mixing Method

1. Mix eggnog, whiskey, vanilla extract, and bitters in a mixing glass.
2. Stir well for 5 to 15 seconds.
3. Pour into a rock glass over a round or square ice cube.
4. Garnish with a cinnamon stick and sprinkle cinnamon on top.

PEPPERMINT OLD FASHIONED

Ingredients

2 oz Brough Brothers Whiskey or any whiskey of your choice

3 dashes of Peychaud's Bitters

½ oz peppermint schnapps

1 candy cane

Mixing Method

1. Mix the whiskey, bitters, and peppermint schnapps in a mixing glass.
2. Stir well for 5 to 15 seconds.
3. Pour into a rock glass over a round or square ice cube.
4. Garnish with a candy cane.

Tips

If you want a more intense peppermint flavor, muddle the candy cane in the bottom of the glass before mixing.

PUMPKIN SPICE OLD FASHIONED

Ingredients

2 oz Maker's Mark Small Batch Whisky

3–4 dashes of black walnut bitters

¼ oz pumpkin spice liqueur

1 orange peel

Mixing Method

1. Mix the whiskey, bitters, and pumpkin spice liqueur in a mixing glass.
2. Stir well for 5 to 15 seconds.
3. Pour into a rock glass over a round or square ice cube.
4. Garnish with orange peel.

Image by wirestock on Freepik

OLD FASHIONED

WITH A TWIST

I have noticed that while I am out in these Houston streets, there have been a lot of twists to the old-fashioned cocktail, and it's not just bitters or syrups. In this section, I created some old-fashioneds that are not bourbon or whiskey-based. These are made with different types of spirits.

Adding different spirits to the old-fashioned brings a twist to this cocktail for those who dislike whiskey or bourbon. Have fun, and I hope you enjoy the taste and the experience of making it.

COCONUT VANILLA RUM OLD FASHIONED

GRAPEFRUIT OLD FASHIONED

JAMAICAN RUM OLD FASHIONED

LYCHEE OLD FASHIONED

RUM OLD FASHIONED

SPICED RUM OLD FASHIONED

TEQUILA OLD FASHIONED

VODKA OLD FASHIONED

BOURBON & BITS

Use your favorite spirits, such as tequilas, rums, and vodka. You are not limited to what I used in this book.

COCONUT VANILLA RUM OLD FASHIONED

Ingredients

2 oz Malibu Rum Original

½ oz vanilla extract

3 dashes of Peychaud's Aromatic Bitters

Mixing Method

1. Mix the Malibu Rum Original, vanilla extract, and bitters in a mixing glass.
2. Stir well for 5 to 10 seconds.
3. Pour into a rock glass over a round or a square ice cube.

GRAPEFRUIT OLD FASHIONED

Ingredients

2 oz Hornitos Black Barrel Tequila

½ oz fresh squeezed Ruby Red grapefruit

½ oz simple syrup

Mixing Method

1. Mix the Hornitos Black Barrel Tequila, Ruby Red grapefruit, and simple syrup in a mixing glass.
2. Stir well for 5 to 10 seconds.
3. Pour into a rock glass over a round or square ice cube.
4. Rim the glass with a grapefruit peel, then place the grapefruit peel in the glass.
5. Garnish with a grapefruit peel.

This cocktail was created by Houston attorney Dan Scarbrough

JAMAICAN RUM OLD FASHIONED

Ingredients

2 oz Appleton Estate 12 Year Rare Casks Rum

½ oz Trader Vic's Macadamia Nut Liqueur

2 dashes of Xocolatl Mole bitters

1 dash Angostura bitters

Mixing Method

1. Mix the Appleton Estate 12 Year Rare Casks Rum, Trader Vic's Macadamia Nut Liqueur, Xocolatl Mole bitters, and Angostura bitters in a mixing glass with ice.
2. Stir well for about 5 to 10 seconds.
3. Pour or strain into a rock glass over a round or square ice cube.

This recipe was created and contributed by mixologist Jubin Shah

LYCHEE OLD FASHIONED

Ingredients

2 oz Suntory Whisky Toki

½ oz Soho Lychee liqueur

3 drops of The Japanese Bitters

2 tablespoons of fresh lychee juice

Mixing Method

1. Mix the Suntory Whisky Toki, Soho Lychee liqueur, Japanese bitters, and lychee juice in a mixing glass.
2. Stir well for 5 to 10 seconds.
3. Pour or strain into a rock glass over a round or square ice cube.
4. Rim the glass with the orange peel, then place the orange peel in the glass.
5. Garnish with lychee fruit and orange peel.

This cocktail was created by Houston attorney Dan Scarbrough

RUM OLD FASHIONED

Ingredients

2 ½ oz Malibu Rum Black

2 dashes of Angostura Bitters

1 dash of triple sec

½ oz simple syrup

Mixing Method

1. Mix the Malibu Rum Black, bitters, triple sec, and simple syrup in a mixing glass.
2. Stir well for 5 to 10 seconds.
3. Pour or strain into a rock glass over a round or square ice cube.

Image by valeria_aksakova on Freepik

SPICED RUM OLD FASHIONED

Ingredients

2 oz Captain Morgan Original Spiced Rum

3 dashes of Peychaud's Bitters

½ oz simple syrup

Mixing Method

1. Mix the Captain Morgan Original Spiced Rum, bitters, and simple syrup in a mixing glass.
2. Stir well for 5 to 10 seconds.
3. Pour into a rock glass over a round or square ice cube.

TEQUILA OLD FASHIONED

Ingredients

2 oz Reposado Tequila

½ oz simple syrup

2–3 dashes of Angostura orange bitters

Mixing Method

1. Mix the Reposado Tequila, simple syrup, and bitters into a mixing glass.
2. Stir well for 5 to 10 seconds.
3. Pour into a rock glass over a round or square ice cube.

Tips

If you like smoked tequila, smoke this cocktail with any flavored wood chips of your choice.

Image by Racool_studio on Freepik

VODKA OLD FASHIONED

Ingredients

2 oz vodka

1–2 tablespoons simple syrup

2–3 dashes of Fee Brothers cranberry bitters

Mixing Method

1. Mix the vodka, simple syrup, and bitters into a mixing glass.
2. Stir well for 5 to 15 seconds.
3. Pour into a rock glass over a round or square ice cube.

I AM JUST HERE
―――――――――――――
FOR THE **DRINKS**

Even though I love all things old-fashioned, I also love whiskey and bourbon. Besides, I can't just write a cocktail book about old-fashioneds and not include some of the famous whiskey and bourbon cocktails. This section will provide you with recipes for well-known cocktails, such as the Kentucky Derby's famous mint julep, a traditional Manhattan, and the Sazerac, a New Orleans favorite, and some of your favorite brunch or dinner cocktails, but I have added whiskey as the liquor.

For those of you who may not like old-fashioneds but love whiskey and bourbon cocktails, this section is for you. Even if you enjoy old-fashioneds like me, sometimes you may be in the mood for something else. You will definitely find a new drink to add to your repertoire.

BOULEVARDIER

BOURBON MARGARITA

THE BOURBON MIMOSA

BOURBON SIDECAR

DALLAS COUNTY WHISKEY MULE

GINGER HIGHBALL

LYCHEE WHISKEY SOUR

MANHATTAN

MINT JULEP

NOT YOUR GRANDMA'S TODDY

PINEAPPLE GINGER WHISKEY SOUR

ROSÈ 75

SAZERAC

TAMARIND WHISKEY SOUR

BOURBON & BITS

The mint julep was first mentioned in print in 1803, and in 1983, the mint julep became the official drink of the Kentucky Derby. To this day, thousands of mint juleps are made during Derby Day throughout the United States.

BOULEVARDIER

Ingredients

1 ½ oz Rye or Whiskey

1 oz Campari

1 oz Martini & Rossi sweet vermouth

Orange slice

Mixing Method

1. Mix the whiskey, bitters, and simple syrup in a mixing glass with ice.
2. Stir well for 10 to 20 seconds.
3. Strain into a chilled glass.
4. Rim the glass with an orange peel.
5. Garnish with an orange peel.

BOURBON & BITS

The Boulevardier is the cousin of the Negroni cocktail, originally made with gin.

BOURBON MARGARITA

Ingredients

2 oz Maker's Mark Kentucky Straight Bourbon Whisky

1 oz Grand Marnier liqueur or triple sec

½ oz freshly squeezed lime juice

½ oz simple syrup or agave syrup

Mixing Method

1. Pour the Maker's Mark Kentucky Straight Bourbon Whisky, Grand Marnier liqueur or triple sec, lime juice, simple syrup, or agave syrup into a cocktail shaker with ice.
2. Shake well for 10 to 20 seconds.
3. Pour into a margarita glass or a glass of your choice.
4. Rim the glass with salt or sugar (optional).

THE BOURBON MIMOSA

Ingredients

2 oz Uncle Nearest 1884 Small Batch Whiskey

½ oz La Marca Prosecco

½ oz orange juice

3 dashes of triple sec

1 Luxardo cherry

Orange peel

Mixing Method

1. Pour the Uncle Nearest 1884 Small Batch Whiskey, La Marca Prosecco, orange juice, and triple sec in a cocktail shaker with ice.
2. Shake well for 10 to 20 seconds.
3. Pour into a flute glass.
4. Garnish with Luxardo cherry and an orange peel.

Tips

Add as much prosecco as you like for the effervescent mimosa.

Image by KamranAydinov on Freepik

BOURBON SIDECAR

Ingredients

2 ½ oz Maker's Mark Kentucky Straight Bourbon Whisky

1 oz Grand Marnier liqueur or Cointreau

½ oz freshly squeezed lemon juice

2 dashes of triple sec

1 lemon peel

1 orange peel

Mixing Method

1. Pour the Maker's Mark Kentucky Straight Bourbon Whisky, Grand Marnier, lemon juice, and triple sec into a cocktail shaker with ice.
2. Shake well for 10 to 20 seconds.
3. Strain into a glass of your choice without ice.
4. Garnish with a fresh lemon peel and an orange peel.

Tips

You can add sugar around the rim of the glass.

DALLAS COUNTY WHISKEY MULE

Ingredients

2 oz Hermann Marshall Dry Country Blended Bourbon Whiskey

2–3 oz of ginger beer

2 tablespoons of freshly squeezed lime juice

1–2 mint leaves

1 small lime

Mixing Method

1. Mix Hermann Marshall Dry County Blended Bourbon Whiskey, ginger beer, and lime juice in a cocktail shaker with crushed ice.
2. Shake well for 10 to 20 seconds.
3. Pour into a copper mug or any glass of your choice.
4. Garnish with a mint leaf.

Tips

Hermann Marshall Dry Country Blended Bourbon Whiskey is a whiskey made in Garland, Texas (Dallas County). Hermann Marshall is the first distillery that was opened and operated in Dallas County. As a Dallas native, I wanted to pay homage to my hometown.

GINGER HIGHBALL

Ingredients

2 oz Maker's Mark Kentucky Straight Bourbon Whisky

½ oz Levels of Grandeur Pineapple Ginger syrup

½ oz ginger beer

Mixing Method

1. Pour the Levels of Grandeur Pineapple Ginger syrup into a highball glass over the ice.
2. Stir well for 5 to 15 seconds.
3. Add Maker's Mark Kentucky Straight Bourbon Whisky and top off with ginger beer.
4. Stir again for 5 to 15 seconds.

Tips

Levels of Grandeur syrups are a premium line of syrups made in Houston, Texas. To purchase a bottle, please visit their website at https://www.levelsofgrandeur.com/.

LYCHEE WHISKEY SOUR

Ingredients

2 oz Uncle Nearest 1884 Small Batch Whiskey

½ oz Levels of Grandeur Lychee Syrup

½ oz freshly squeezed lemon juice

Mixing Method

1. Pour Uncle Nearest 1884 Small Batch Whiskey, Levels of Grandeur Lychee syrup, and lemon juice into a cocktail shaker with ice.
2. Shake well for 10 to 20 seconds.
3. Strain into a rock glass over ice.
4. Garnish with a lemon peel and lychee fruit.

BOURBON & BITS

Levels of Grandeur syrups are a premium line of syrups made in Houston, Texas. To purchase a bottle, please visit their website at https://www.levelsofgrandeur.com/.

MANHATTAN

Ingredients

2 oz rye or whiskey

2–3 dashes of Peychaud's bitters

½ oz Martini & Rossi sweet vermouth

3 dashes of triple sec

1 Luxardo cherry

Orange peel

Mixing Method

1. Mix the rye whiskey, bitters, vermouth, and triple sec in a mixing glass with ice.
2. Stir well for 5 to 15 seconds.
3. Strain and then pour into a glass of your choice.
4. Garnish with Luxardo cherry and an orange peel.

MINT JULEP

Ingredients

2 oz Maker's Mark Kentucky Straight Bourbon Whisky

½ oz simple syrup or 2–3 sugar cubes

4–8 fresh mint leaves

Mixing Method

1. Pour the simple syrup and add the mint leaves into the rock glass or a traditional mint julep glass.
2. Use a muddler and muddle the mint leaves mixed with the simple syrup.
3. Add Maker's Mark Kentucky Straight Bourbon Whisky.
4. Add crushed ice and stir well.
5. Garnish with a mint leaf.

Tips

The purpose of muddling the mint leaves is to release the oil and aroma of the mint. If you use sugar cubes instead of simple syrup, muddle the sugar cubes with the mint leaves.

NOT YOUR GRANDMA'S TODDY

Ingredients

2 oz Old Dominick's Memphis Toddy

½ oz honey

1 peppermint stick

½ oz fresh squeezed lemon juice

1 oz whiskey

Mixing Method

1. Pour Old Dominick's Memphis Toddy, honey, lemon juice, and whiskey into a mug.
2. Stir well for about 5 to 15 seconds.
3. Garnish with a peppermint stick.

Tips

You can heat this cocktail over the stove or in the microwave. You can also give it a different flavor by smoking it.

PINEAPPLE GINGER WHISKEY SOUR

Ingredients

2 ½ oz Maker's Mark Kentucky Straight Bourbon Whisky

½ oz Levels of Grandeur Pineapple Ginger Sour

½ oz orange juice

2 dashes of triple sec

1 small lime

Mixing Method

1. Pour the Maker's Mark Kentucky Straight Bourbon Whisky, pineapple ginger sour, orange juice, and triple sec into a cocktail shaker with ice.
2. Shake well for 10 to 20 seconds.
3. Pour into a glass of your choice.
4. Garnish with a fresh lime.

ROSÉ 75

Ingredients

2 oz Penelope Rosé Cask Finished Bourbon

¼ oz champagne or sparkling wine

1 lemon peel

Mixing Method

1. Pour the Penelope Rose Cask Finish and champagne or sparkling wine into a cocktail shaker with ice.
2. Shake well for 10 to 20 seconds.
3. Pour into a flute glass.
4. Garnish with a lemon peel.

SAZERAC

Ingredients

2 oz Hartman's Straight Rye Whiskey

¼ oz Absinthe

1 sugar cube

3 dashes of Peychaud's bitters

1 lemon peel

Mixing Method

1. Rinse the rock glass with the absinthe and then remove the extra liquid.
2. Add the sugar cube to a mixing glass and muddle the sugar.
3. Add the bitters, whiskey, and ice.
4. Stir well.
5. Strain into the glass.

BOURBON & BITS

Sazerac is the cousin of the old-fashioned and was created in New Orleans. *Laissez les bons temps rouler:* Let the good times roll!

TAMARIND WHISKEY SOUR

Ingredients

2 oz Uncle Nearest 1884 Small Batch Whiskey

½ oz Levels of Grandeur Tamarind Syrup

½ oz freshly squeezed lemon juice

1 lemon

Mixing Method

1. Pour the Uncle Nearest 1884 Small Batch Whiskey, tamarind syrup, and lemon juice into a cocktail shaker with ice.
2. Shake well for 10 to 20 minutes.
3. Pour into a glass of your choice.
4. Garnish with a lemon peel.

ACKNOWLEDGMENTS

First, I want to thank God for giving me the vision to create this book. I have done many things but never thought I would write a book about cocktails.

Thank you to my mother for always allowing me to follow my dreams and giving me the space to act on those dreams, no matter how unorthodox they are. I am grateful for the tools you and daddy instilled in me to become successful. You always told me I was extraordinary and never average, so here I am, and I refuse to quit.

Thank you to my best friend, LaToya Sheals. We are on our way to taking over the world, Pinky!

Thank you to my "werk bestie," Ashleigh Gardner-Cormier, for allowing me to bounce ideas with you and being my creative ying.

Thank you to Dan Scarborough and Jubin Shah for your creative contributions to this book.

Thank you to Walter Carrier for introducing me to the world of whiskey. I was trying to do a simple Instagram page about old-fashioneds, and you stepped in and

showed me that there is an entire world that needs to be explored.

Thank you to Samantha Frazier for coming up with the book's title. I have always told you that you have the best ideas for naming things.

Thank you to RJ and Candace Blue for their genuine guidance and support. I appreciate the conversations, the encouraging words, and the mentorship that you both have provided to me.

Thanks to *Say Bruh* for believing in me and being my taste tester. When I began this journey, you saw the vision while I was trying to map out the idea. You encouraged me to tune out the negative opinions and comments, to think outside the box, and reminded me to continue to dream bigger.

Lastly, thanks to everyone who decided to join me on this journey. I appreciate you all for supporting my events, tasting or trying an old-fashioned, and just being there as needed. Cheers!

REFERENCES

1. Glass, Jeremy. "A Short and Sweet History of the Old-Fashioned." *Thrillist*, 13 Apr. 2015, www.thrillist.com/vice/history-and-origin-of-the-old-fashioned-cocktail.

2. Endolyn, Osayi. "The Smoldering History of Smoke in Cocktails." Tales of the Cocktail Foundation, 9 Apr. 2020, www.talesofthecocktail.org/history/smoldering-history-smoke-cocktails

3. History of Tom Bullock, The Life and Legacy of Tom Bullock : GoToLouisville.com Official Travel Source

4. "A Complete History of the Mint Julep." Town & Country, 18 Apr. 2022, www.townandcountrymag.com/leisure/drinks/news/a6026/history-of-the-mint-julep.

5. **Danval Scarbrough** is a lawyer by trade and a native Houstonian. He believes that Houston is closed and isn't accepting new residents at this time. Dan is a crafty type of person and became interested in mixology after he started law school at Thurgood Marshall School of Law. He has been mixing privately for special events for years; however, he does not consider himself a professional by any means. His favorite drinks are simple ones, but he does like playing with flavors. Dan's favorite bourbon is Eagle Rare, and his favorite cocktail is an old-fashioned made with Bulleit Rye, Angostura Bitters, Turbinado syrup, and Luxardo Cherry.

6. **Jubin Shah** is a Houston bartender, working since 2012 in everything from small, family-owned restaurants and college nightclubs to fine dining and upscale lounges. With simplicity trending, he believes cocktails should be fun, classy, and approachable by everyone. He is currently the co-owner of Split Base Creative, a beverage agency that focuses on promoting equitable business and supporting the community. Cheers!

ABOUT THE AUTHOR

Brandi Lowery, the Old Fashioned Barrister, is a Dallas native but currently resides in Houston, Texas, where she is a licensed attorney. She is an executive bourbon steward and an Edu-taster for Whiskey University. She holds several whiskey certifications and is well-known within the whiskey community.

She has been featured in several magazines, such as Voyage Magazine, Shout Out Magazine, and Canvas Rebel Magazine. She loves to make old-fashioneds in her kitchen, teach others about the history of whiskey, and entertain guests by showing off her knowledge and skills.

www.ingramcontent.com/pod-product-compliance
Lightning Source LLC
Chambersburg PA
CBHW041422010526
44119CB00015B/344